Rest in HIM

Scriptures for Daily Peace

Dr. C. White-Elliott

www.clfpublishing.org
909.315.3161

Copyright © 2021 by Cassundra White-Elliott.

All rights reserved. No portion of this book may be reproduced, stored in a retrieval system, or transmitted by any form or any means electronically, photocopied, recorded, or any other except for brief quotations in printed reviews, without the prior permission of the publisher.

Cover design by Senir Design. Contact info: info@senirdesign.com

ISBN #978-1-945102-68-4

Printed in the United States of America.

Dedication

For *Mi Amour*,
during a trying season
of unrest

Table of Contents

Accusations	9
Anger	10
Animosity	11
Anxiety	12
Bitterness	13
Boredom	14
Broken-Hearted	15
Burdened	16
Calmness	17
Compassion	18
Confusion	19
Consideration	20
Controlling	21
Counsel	22
Courage	23
Covetousness	24
Death	25
Depression	26
Despair	27
Disappointment	28
Envy	29
Faithfulness	30
Fear	31
Finances	32
Forgiveness	33
Friendly	34

Gentleness	35
Giving	36
Gluttony	37
Goodness	38
Gratitude	39
Greed	40
Grief	41
Guilt	42
Happiness	43
Hardship	44
Hardened Heart	45
Honesty	46
Hope	47
Hopelessness	48
Humility	49
Indignation	50
Jealousy	51
Joy	52
Kindness	53
Lasciviousness	54
Laughter	55
Laziness	56
Loneliness	57
Longsuffering	58
Loss	59
Love	60

Lust	61
Lying	62
Misery	63
Modesty	64
Obstinate	65
Oppression	66
Overwhelmed	67
Patience	68
Peace	69
Possessiveness	70
Pride	71
Procrastination	72
Promiscuity	73
Rebellious	74
Regret	75
Relationships	76
Remorse	77
Reprobate Mind	78
Respect	79
Responsibility	80
Restlessness	81
Revenge	82
Self-Control	83
Selfish	84
Servitude	85
Shame	86
Sorrow	87

Temptation	88
Thievery	89
Tolerance	90
Transgression	91
Treasure	92
Trust	93
Trustworthy	94
Truth	95
Value	96
Victorious	97
Victory	98
Weeping	99
Weakness	100
Weary	101
Wickedness	102
Wonderful	103
Worry	104
The Gift of Salvation	105
About the Author	111

Accusations

Refrain from casting accusations towards others in moments of frustration. Our objective should always be to keep the peace among all people at all times. And, when accusations are hurled towards us, we should take them in stride. Do not retaliate. The Lord will rescue and defend us.

So, <u>Rest in Him</u>.

"Yet Michael the archangel, when contending with the devil he disputed about the body of Moses, durst not bring against him a railing accusation, but said, 'The Lord rebuke thee'."
(Jude 1:19, KJV)

Anger

Anger is a natural human emotion that we all experience at one time or another. However, anger must be controlled at all times, so we do not run the risk of sinning by going too far. When you have a moment of anger, be still and Rest in Him, allowing the Lord to calm you down, for His Word says,

"'Be angry, and do not sin': do not let the sun go down on your wrath."
(Ephesians 4:26, NKJV)

Animosity

Do not hold animosity in your heart from past deeds that were committed against you. Exercise forgiveness, even for the most horrendous offenses. Your mind will be freer, and you will walk in the peace of God.

"Be kind to one another, compassionate, forgiving each other, just as God in Christ also has forgiven you."
(Eph 4:32, NASB)

Anxiety

Anxiety can rise up within us at a moment's notice. However, we must learn to quell that emotion lest it get the best of us. To diffuse anxiety, enter into prayer and make your requests known before the Lord. Share with Him your innermost thoughts, desires, fears, concerns, needs, etc.

"Do not be anxious about anything, but in every situation, by prayer and petition, with thanksgiving, present your requests to God."
(Philippians 4:6, NIV)

Bitterness

The root of bitterness grows deep, and from it grows other dangerous conditions, such as procrastination, murder, hatred, and contention. Be careful to not allow bitterness to set in. Remain free in Him, keeping the enemy from gaining a foothold.

"Let all bitterness, and wrath, and anger, and clamour, and evil speaking, be put away from you, with all malice."
(Eph 4:31, KJV)

Boredom

Find something positive to do with your free time. Counsel someone. Feed the hungry. Encourage the disenfranchised and the marginalized. Volunteer at a youth or senior citizen center. Spread the gospel to the lost. Serve at your local church. If you consult the Lord, He will give you an assignment.

"Laziness brings on deep sleep, and an idle soul will suffer hunger."
(Proverbs 19:15, BSB)

Broken-Hearted

The Lord will always give comfort to the broken-hearted. He will never leave you destitute. He will never forsake you, especially when you are experiencing a low moment in your life. But, you must turn to Him, for your healing, and He will lift you up.

"The LORD is near to the brokenhearted and saves the crushed in spirit."
(Psalm 34:18, ESV)

Burdened

When your heart is heavy and you require a reprieve, the Lord is always nearby to comfort you and to carry your burdens. You just have to release it into His hands.

"Come to me, all who labor and are heavy laden, and I will give you rest. Take my yoke upon you, and learn from me, for I am gentle and lowly in heart, and you will find rest for your souls. For my yoke is easy, and my burden is light."
(Matthew 11:28-30, ESV)

Calmness

Although it may be easier said than done, it is always best to exercise calmness in all situations. When you become agitated, the situation becomes heightened and can easily take a deadly turn. Is that really your desire?

"Fear not, for I am with you; be not dismayed, for I am your God; I will strengthen you, I will help you, I will uphold you with my righteous right hand."
(Isaiah 41:10, ESV)

Compassion

Compassion is rarely offered between people. It is an emotion that is rarely shared when needed. If people were more compassionate, we could have healthier societies and a better world.

"Be kind and compassionate to one another, forgiving each other, just as in Christ God forgave you."

(Ephesian 4:32, NIV)

Confusion

Being Christlike, refrain from causing confusion and from getting involved in confusion. When confusion rears its ugly head, go in the other direction!

"For God is not the author of confusion, but of peace, as in all churches of the saints."

(I Corinthians 14:33, KJV)

Consideration

In all you do, look outside yourself and consider the needs of others. We all need assistance at one time or another. Today, just may be the day for you to assist someone else. They are waiting for you, so lend a helping hand.

"Let each of you look not only to his own interests, but also to the interests of others."
(Philippians 2:4, ESV)

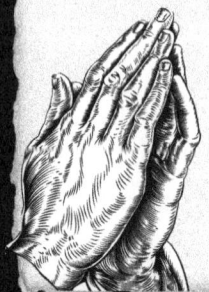

Controlling

A controlling spirit is not of the Lord. It is a spirit of the adversary, being used to sow seeds of discord and to do his bidding.

A controlling spirit usurps a person's autonomy over his/her own life. God gave us free will; therefore, we should permit one another to exercise it.

"Now I exhort you, brethren, by the name of our Lord Jesus Christ, that you all agree and that there be no divisions among you, but that you be made complete in the same mind and in the same judgment."

(I Cor. 1:10, NASB)

Counsel

Anytime you encounter difficulties in life, seek godly counsel when making a decision. Those who possess the wisdom of God can provide godly counsel according to that which is written within the Holy Writ and that which is given by the Holy Spirit.

"...and in abundance of counselors there is victory."
(Proverbs 24:6, ESV)

Courage

Courage seemingly belongs to the brave. However, that is not completely true. If you place your hope in the Lord, He will give you courage. That courage is simply the ability to believe God is able to do exceeding abundantly above all we can ask or think. We don't look to ourselves for things to happen. Instead, we to the Lord.

"So be strong and courageous, all you who put your hope in the LORD!"
(Psalm 31:34, NLT)

Covetousness

Do not look upon what belongs to another and desire it for yourself. What God has for you is for you. What God has given another is for that person. Period!

"You are jealous and covet [what others have] and your lust goes unfulfilled; so you murder. You are envious and cannot obtain [the object of your envy]; so you fight and battle. You do not have because you do not ask [it of God]."

(James 4:2, AB)

Death

Death can be one of the most difficult occurrences we face, especially the death of a loved one. However, we can take comfort in knowing that our saved loved ones are truly in a better condition as they Rest in the bosom of the Lord.

"We are confident, I say, and willing rather to be absent from the body, and to be present with the Lord."
(II Corinthians 5:8, KJV)

Depression

Depression is a dark, bottomless abyss with no end in sight to the sorrow that is being experienced. You may feel as though you are without a lifeline. But, the devil is a liar! Your lifeline is Jesus Christ. Reach up to Him, allowing Him to grab your hand. He will lift you up. When He does,
<u>Rest in Him</u>.

"The righteous cry out, and the Lord hears them; he delivers them from all their troubles. The Lord is close to the brokenhearted and saves those who are crushed in spirit."
(Psalm 34:17-18, NIV)

Despair

At times, trouble seems to circle about us, waiting to pounce when we least expect it. But, do not despair. Hold your head high and look toward the hills, knowing your help comes from the Lord. He will certainly be there in your times of trouble.

"We are troubled on every side, yet not distressed; we are perplexed, but not in despair."
(II Cor. 4:8, KJV)

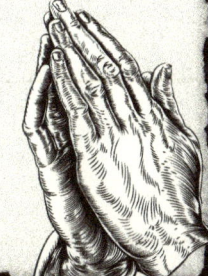

Disappointment

Disappointment in this life is inevitable. But, the pleasures of life can be more abundant when you learn to see the silver lining in each situation. God has great things in store for you. Keep watch for the great things. Expect them. Seize every opportunity.

"Now hope does not disappoint, because the love of God has been poured out in our hearts by the Holy Spirit who was given to us."
(Romans 5:5, NKJV)

Envy

Do not flaunt yourself about, provoking others to envy you. Also, do not stand in envy of others. We should all bless the name of the Lord, knowing He is no respecter of persons. What He does for one, He can do for all.

*"Let us not become conceited,
provoking one another,
envying one another."*
(Galatians 5:26, NKJV)

Faithfulness

Be faithful unto death of all God places in your hands. Be diligent in all He has called you to do. Then, when you have proven yourself to the Lord, He will reward you with more responsibility.

"His lord said to him, 'Well done, good and faithful servant; you have been faithful over a few things, I will make you ruler over many things. Enter into the joy of your lord'."

(Matthew 25:23, NKJV)

Fear

When you find your stomach twisting in knots because fear has taken ahold of you, and you cannot seem to shake it... When you cannot seem to find the courage you need to break free from fear's grip... <u>Rest in Him</u>, knowing,

"For God hath not given us the spirit of fear; but of power, and of love, and of a sound mind."

(II Timothy 1:7, KJV)

Finances

Financial stability breeds freedom and peace of mind. Do not allow financial struggles to overwhelm you. Take control today by obtaining assistance. Do not allow the enemy to cause you to be embarrassed. Take back the driver's seat and breathe easily.

"You have sown much, and bring in little; You eat, but do not have enough; You drink, but you are not filled with drink; You clothe yourselves, but no one is warm; And he who earns wages, Earns wages to put into a bag with holes."

(Haggai 5:6, NKJV)

Forgiveness

For many, forgiveness is a struggle. Understand this- if you want the Father to forgive you of your wrongdoing, you must forgive others. Release them from your charge, and God will release you from His.

"For if you forgive men their trespasses, your heavenly Father will also forgive you."
(Matthew 6:14, NKJV)

Friendly

Friendliness is the requirement for friendships to manifest. Friends are drawn by kind words, kind gestures, a smile, and a tender heart. Jesus had a great number of followers because of the compassion He showed towards mankind. He was not fearful of showing His tender side. As a result, crowds gathered around Him.

"A man who has friends must himself be friendly, But there is a friend who sticks closer than a brother."
(Proverbs 18:24, NKJV)

Gentleness

In the harsh, cold world in which we reside, where tensions run deep and harshness runs rampant, allow gentleness to permeate the atmosphere, causing the negativity to dissipate. Allow a gentle spirit to flow from you when you enter into a room. People will be thankful for your presence because you bring the "light" with you.

"Let your gentleness be known to all men. The Lord is at hand."
(Philippians 4:5, NKJV)

Giving

Of all the Lord has blessed you with, give. If He blesses you with knowledge, share. If He blesses you with love, share. If He blesses you with free time, share. If He blesses you with finances, share. Be a giver, and watch the Lord bless you ever the more.

"Give, and it shall be given unto you; good measure, pressed down, and shaken together, and running over, shall men give into your bosom. For with the same measure that ye mete withal it shall be measured to you again."

(Luke 6:38, KJV)

Gluttony

The cares of the world can overwhelm us, wearing us down because we took on more than we were able to handle. Watch your intake. Don't over do it. All things in moderation. Partake of healthy limits.

"But beware in your souls that your hearts never grow cold with gluttony and with drunkenness and with the cares of the world, and suddenly it shall come upon you that day."

(Luke 21:34, ABPE)

Goodness

The Lord supplies us with goodness, and He is not in short supply of it. As the Lord's goodness (grace) and His love (mercy) surround us, we would do well to spread grace and mercy to others, demonstrating the love of God.

"Surely your goodness and love will follow me all the days of my life, and I will dwell in the house of the LORD forever."
(Psalm 23:6, NIV)

Gratitude

The Lord has truly been good to us all, and we owe Him our gratitude. Sing praises unto the Lord, and show one another kindness and gentleness.

"Let the word of Christ richly dwell within you, with all wisdom teaching and admonishing one another with psalms, hymns, and spiritual songs, singing with thankfulness in your hearts to God."
(Colossians 3:16, NASB)

Greed

The Lord is the gracious giver of all good gifts. Remembering from whom all blessings flow can free us from the spirit of greed. Instead, we should be infused with thankfulness, knowing it is the Lord God who gives us the power to gain wealth and not we ourselves.

"But He said to them, 'Beware, and be on your guard against every form of greed; for not even when one is affluent does his life consist of his possessions'."
(Luke 12:15, NASB)

Grief

When you experience grief, the Lord will be your comfort. He will cradle you in His arms, for He is the god of all comfort.

"But you, God, see the trouble of the afflicted; you consider their grief and take it in hand. The victims commit themselves to you; you are the helper of the fatherless."
(Psalm 10:14, NIV)

Guilt

The devil, our adversary, will always attempt to give us a guilt trip about past and present deeds. He wants us to wallow in guilt, stripping us of our joy. But, we are not fooled by Satan's devices. <u>Rest in the Lord</u>. He will give us peace.

"There is therefore now no condemnation to those who are in Christ Jesus, who do not walk according to the flesh, but according to the Spirit."
(Romans 8:1, NKJV)

Happiness

The promises of God provide happiness and joy. Always look for the best in every situation. Keep a positive outlook. Doing so will keep your spirit man lifted, even when the world around you sings a sad song.

"The hopes of the godly result in happiness, but the expectations of the wicked come to nothing."
(Proverbs 10:28, NLT)

Hardship

Do not allow hardship to deter you from your ministry. Stay the course and count it all joy as you face various trials. Keep a smile on your face, and keep your head lifted.

"But you, be sober in all things, endure hardship, do the work of an evangelist, fulfill your ministry."
(II Timothy 4:5, BSB)

Hardened Heart

Be mindful of how you respond to the circumstances you encounter. Extreme and prolonged anger, disappointment, and sadness can lead to a hardened heart. Allow your heart to be supple and not overwhelmed with the issues of life.

"And Jesus, aware of this, said to them, "Why are you discussing the fact that you have no bread? Do you not yet perceive or understand? Are your hearts hardened? Having eyes do you not see, and having ears do you not hear? And do you not remember?"
(Mark 8:17-18, BSB)

Honesty

Honesty and integrity go hand in hand. When a person is honest, he/she walks in integrity. When a person walks in integrity, he/she is honest. These characteristics should be beholden of believers who call upon the name of the Lord.

"May integrity and honesty protect me, for I put my hope in you."
(Psalm 25:21, NLT)

Hope

Keep your hope strong by reading God's Word. It will encourage you even in your darkest hour. When you feel down and your spirits are low, allow your hope in God's promises to allow you to press forward in Him.

"May the God of hope fill you with all joy and peace as you trust in him, so that you may overflow with hope by the power of the Holy Spirit."
(Romans 15:13, NIV)

Hopelessness

When our friends and family members are overcome with hopelessness, not wanting to look forward to the possibilities of tomorrow, we must encourage their hearts in an effort to pull them out of their depression.

"Praise be to the God and Father of our Lord Jesus Christ, the Father of compassion and the God of all comfort, who comforts us in all our troubles, so that we can comfort those in any trouble with the comfort we ourselves receive from God."

(II Corinthians 1:3-4)

Humility

With all humility, honor the Lord and those who serve Him *without* respect to titles and positions. Rid yourself of prideful tendencies, knowing if it were not for the grace and mercy of the Lord, where would you be?

> *"The fear of the LORD is the instruction of wisdom; and before honour is humility."*
> (Proverbs 15:33, KJV)

Indignation

Do not wear indignation upon your countenance. Leave the wicked evildoers to the Lord. He will recompense.

"I remembered Your judgments of old, O LORD, And have comforted myself. Indignation has taken hold of me because of the wicked, who forsake Your law."
(Psalm 119:52-53, NKJV)

Jealousy

As believers, we do not walk in the spirit of jealousy, allowing it to fill our hearts. Nor, do we carry selfish ambition, trying to outperform or outrank others. A jealous personality will halt one's progress rather than provide elevation.

"But if you are bitterly jealous and there is selfish ambition in your heart, don't cover up the truth with boasting and lying."
(James 3:14, NLT)

Joy

The sorrows we experience are temporary. But, the joy of the Lord is everlasting. Rejoice in the Lord, finding strength, comfort, peace, fulfillment, and understanding.

"Do not sorrow, for the joy of the LORD is your strength."
(Nehemiah 8:10c, NKJV)

Kindness

Show kindness to all people, those you know and strangers alike. A kind spirit gives relief, breeds joy everlasting, and demonstrates a gentle spirit. A kind word quells anger. A kind word halts a suicidal thought. A kind word breathes life into people who are breathing their last breaths. Be kind. Be tender. Be loving.

"We prove ourselves by our purity, our understanding, our patience, our kindness, by the Holy Spirit within us, and by our sincere love."
(II Corinthians 6:6, NLT)

Lasciviousness

Lasciviousness is the work of the enemy through a vessel that has been given over to greed and malice. If you find yourself crossing the line of contentment to always seeking more and more without a valid purpose, you may be treading on dangerous ground. Give your desires to the Lord, as He will supply what is needed in the proper season.

"Who being past feeling have given themselves over unto lasciviousness, to work all uncleanness with greediness."
(Ephesians 4:19, KJV)

Laughter

When your heart is heavy and the tears seem as though they will never cease falling, unexpectantly, the Lord will replace your sorrow with laughter.
In a moment's notice, you will be able to <u>Rest in Him</u>, as

*"He will yet fill your mouth with laughing,
And your lips with rejoicing."*
(Job 8:21, NKJV)

Laziness

There is a time for work and a time for rest. We must work while it is day. When the Lord assigns a task, be responsible and full of vigor to carry out the task. When the task has been completed, take your rest. When it is time for the next task, rise up and accomplish it.

"The hand of the diligent will rule,
But the lazy hand will be put
to forced labor."

(Proverbs 12:24, NASB)

Loneliness

When you feel as though the world has gone silent and there is no one to give you physical comfort and provide you with much needed company, Rest in Him. Call on His name, knowing you are truly not alone.

"Even if my father and mother abandon me, the LORD will hold me close."
(Psalm 27:10, NLT)

Longsuffering

Even when you may not always do or say the right thing or portray the right attitude, the Lord is yet longsuffering, gentle, and kind-hearted toward us. Can we not demonstrate those same qualities toward one another?

Rest in Him, realizing,

"The Lord is not slack concerning his promise, as some men count slackness; but is longsuffering to us-ward, not willing that any should perish, but that all should come to repentance."

(II Peter 3:9, KJV)

Loss

In life, you may suffer loss and feel the weight of it, causing inner turmoil. But if the trade off of the loss is spiritual gain, what have you really lost? If the loss causes you to seek the Lord, you have gained a stronger relationship with the Father.

"Yet indeed I also count all things loss for the excellence of the knowledge of Christ Jesus my Lord, for whom I have suffered the loss of all things, and count them as rubbish, that I may gain Christ"
(Philippians 3:8, NKJV)

Love

At times, we place too much focus on the cares of this world. The more time we focus on worldly things, the less focus we place on God. There is a cost to pay for the attention we give. We should always seek to love the Lord.

"Love not the world, neither the things that are in the world. If any man love the world, the love of the Father is not in him."

(I John 2:15, KJV)

Lust

Lust can manifest itself in various forms, not only sexually. Regardless of your personal struggle with lust, the Lord can free you from unclean desires and practices, as you learn to shift your desires to the things of God. Keeping the words of the Lord at the forefront of your mind can help you make needed change.

"But I tell you that anyone who looks at a woman lustfully has already committed adultery with her in his heart."
(Matthew 5:28, NIV)

Lying

Put away lying for it is an unbecoming personality trait, and it does not bring glory to God. If it is truly an area in which you struggle, learn to be quiet, not giving yourself an opportunity to speak untruths. <u>Rest in Him</u> as you learn to use your words to please the Father because

"Lying lips are abomination to the LORD: but they that deal truly are his delight."

(Proverbs 12:22, KJV)

Misery

Greed or a desire for more and more and more can lead to the spirit of misery when the desire goes unfulfilled. Ask yourself, "Has God met my needs?" and "Is this thing I seek after really what God has for me?" Seek the Lord, and He will answer your concern. Find your Rest in Him when thinking,

"How miserable I am! I feel like the fruit picker after the harvest who can find nothing to eat. Not a cluster of grapes or a single early fig can be found to satisfy my hunger."
(Micah 7:1, NLT)

Modesty

Be modest in all you do. Being sober minded and level headed will keep you vigilant, aware of impending or approaching danger, so you will not be caught unaware.

"Be sober, be vigilant; because your adversary the devil walks about like a roaring lion, seeking whom he may devour."
(I Peter 5:8, NKJV)

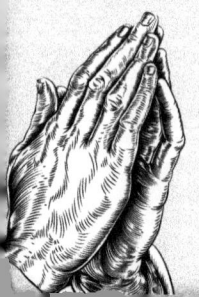

Obstinate

Being obstinate is to have a stubborn spirit regarding your opinion or behavior, which can lead to distasteful and unbecoming behavior. Be willing to allow the Spirit of the Lord to lead you into all righteousness and show you how to have a more amenable personality, one that will allow you to receive instruction and to work in concert with others.

"But they refused to pay attention; stubbornly they turned their backs and covered their ears."
(Zechariah 7:11, NIV)

Oppression

When the pressures of life are weighing down on you and you do not know where to turn for a release or a breath of fresh air, take your <u>Rest in Him</u>, for He cares for you and will not permit you to be overcome.

"The LORD also will be a refuge for the oppressed, A refuge in times of trouble."
(Psalm 9:9, NKJV)

Overwhelmed

Never allow the pressures that are entangled within this world system to allow you to be overwhelmed with grief, fear, sadness, gloom, or despair. In trying times, continue to look to the Lord for He is your ever-present help in the times of trouble. Find your peace as you
<u>Rest in Him</u>.

"There they are, overwhelmed with dread, where there was nothing to fear. For God has scattered the bones of those who besieged you. You put them to shame, for God has despised them."
(Psalm 53:5, BSB)

Patience

Patience leads to endurance, then kindness, then to being a peacemaker. A patient person can go much farther in life than a person who is always in a hurry and lacks due diligence to stay the course when completing a complicated task. When you feel patience is not your strong suit, take your Rest in Him, for

"Better is the end of a thing than the beginning thereof: and the patient in spirit is better than the proud in spirit."
(Ecclesiastes 7:8, KJV)

Peace

In a time when people are losing their minds due to their involvement in chaotic situations, be thankful that the Lord of Comfort will surround you with His peace. Carry it with you in all situations.

"Now may the Lord of peace himself give you peace at all times and in every way. The Lord be with all of you."

(II Thess. 3:16, NIV)

Possessiveness

Do not hold tightly to possessions that have no eternal value. Seek the Kingdom of God and that which you desire, you shall have.

"But understand this, that in the last days there will come times of difficulty. For people will be lovers of self, lovers of money, proud, arrogant, abusive, disobedient to their parents, ungrateful, unholy, heartless, unappeasable, slanderous, without self-control, brutal, not loving good, treacherous, reckless, swollen with conceit, lovers of pleasure rather than lovers of God, having the appearance of godliness, but denying its power. Avoid such people."

(II Timothy 3:1-5, ESV)

Pride

The world system pumps up people to revel in their successes, which leads to the spirit of pride. Pride leads to destruction, but destruction can be avoided when pride is replaced with humility. Believing all gifts and talents come from God should assist in developing humility.

"For all that is in the world, the lust of the flesh, and the lust of the eyes, and the pride of life, is not of the Father, but is of the world."
(I John 2:16, KJV)

Procrastination

Never put off the work of the Lord for tomorrow when you are capable of completing the assignment today. Procrastination will gain you nothing! Be diligent in carrying out each task, for

"The soul of the sluggard craves and gets nothing, while the soul of the diligent is richly supplied."
(Proverbs 13:4, ESV)

Promiscuity

Keep your body pure from all unclean sexual activity, knowing your body is the temple of the Holy Spirit. When you are facing a moment of weakness, turn your attention to the Lord, as you

"Flee from sexual immorality. Every other sin a person commits is outside the body, but the sexually immoral person sins against his own body."
(I Corinthians 6:18, ESV)

Rebellious

Rebelling against authority is a quick way to suffer negative consequences. When you rebel against God, there are consequences for each offence. God loves you, and He will provide ample opportunities for you to see the error of your ways and give you time to make the needed correction. When you notice that you place your will over God's will for your life, you are walking in rebellion. Lay aside that weight and <u>Rest in Him</u>, for He cares for you.

"Many times He rescued them, but they were bent on rebellion sank down in their iniquity."
(Psalm 106:43, BSB)

Regret

Undoubtedly, in life you will have regrets. Nevertheless, do not allow your regrets to weigh you down and make you overcome with grief. Take your regrets to the Lord and repent of all wrongdoings, knowing He cares for you.

"For godly sorrow produces repentance leading to salvation, not to be regretted; but the sorrow of the world produces death."
(II Cor. 7:10, NKJV)

Relationships

Oftentimes, we focus on building and strengthening our horizontal relationships with the people around us. However, the vertical relationship we have with our heavenly Father is of the utmost importance and should be attended to daily. Even when you do not know the right words to say in every circumstance, <u>Rest in Him</u>. He knows your heart.

"Though one may be overpowered by another, two can withstand him. And a threefold cord is not quickly broken."
(Ecclesiastes 4:12, NKJV)

Remorse

It is a natural response to feel remorse when you have made a misstep in your life, especially when you have a heart that desires to please God. Do not wallow in remorse. Go to the Father and repent. Then, <u>Rest in Him</u> as He forgives your iniquity.

Say to Him, *"Purify me from my sins, and I will be clean; wash me, and I will be whiter than snow."*
(Psalm 51:7, NLT)

Reprobate Mind

Being left to walk in your own way when you refuse to attend to God's will and His ways is God's method of leaving you to your own devices. Is your life better with God or without Him? Can you manage on your own as an unbeliever would? Choose to walk with the Lord today. <u>Rest in Him</u>, knowing He has your best interest at heart.

"And even as they did not like to retain God in their knowledge, God gave them over to a reprobate mind, to do those things which are not convenient."
(Romans 1:28, KJV)

Respect

Respect breeds respect. When you demonstrate self-respect and give respect to others as well, respect will be shown unto you.

"Show respect for all people [treat them honorably], love the brotherhood [of believers], fear God, honor the king."
(I Peter 2:17, AB)

Responsibility

Each of us has been given an earthly responsibility - a calling – within the earth realm. Take heed of your calling and carry out your responsibility with all diligence. Your reward in heaven will be well worth it, and you will hear the Lord say, "Well done, my good and faithful servant."

"And so, brothers, select seven men who are well respected and are full of the Spirit and wisdom. We will give them this responsibility."
(Acts 6:3, NLT)

Restlessness

Lying awake at night, tossing and turning, with sleep evading you, hour by hour, because your mind is not at ease is not the will of God. Place your confidence in Him. Give Him your cares and concerns. Find your <u>Rest in Him.</u>

"Come to Me, all you who labor and are heavy laden, and I will give you rest."
(Matthew 11:28, NKJV)

Revenge

When someone has wronged you, and you have it in your heart to repay the wrong that was done, STOP!
<u>Rest in the Lord</u>, because He is already prepared to deal with the wrong that was committed against you.

"For we know Him who said, 'Vengeance is Mine, I will repay,' says the Lord. And again, "The LORD will judge His people'."
(Hebrew 10:30, NKJV)

Self-Control

Never allow anyone to cause you to act out of character. Remember, you are a child of the King! Act like it. Talk like it. Walk like it. No one controls you. Retain your self-control at all times.

"But the fruit of the Spirit is love, joy, peace, longsuffering, kindness, goodness, faithfulness, gentleness, self-control. Against such there is no law."
(Galatians 5:22-23, NKJV)

Selfish

Placing your own desires above everyone else's at all times and at any cost is selfish behavior. Strive to be selfless, thinking of others in their time of need. Life is not a competition. God has more than enough to bless us all.

"For where jealousy and selfish ambition exist, there is disorder [unrest, rebellion] and every evil thing and morally degrading practice."

(James 3:16, AB)

Servitude

Our service belongs to the King of Kings. We answer to Him and Him alone. Therefore, we are required to bring our body (our actions) in line with His Word.

"But I chastise my body, and bring it into servitude, lest by any means, having preached to others -- I myself may become disapproved."
(I Corinthians 9:27, YLT)

Shame

Hidden sin brings shame upon one's countenance. Repentance brings freedom from shame. Do not allow shame to wear you down and make you feel less than the person you are.

"But we have renounced the hidden things of shame, not walking in craftiness, nor falsifying the word of God, but by manifestation of the truth, commending ourselves to every man's conscience before God."
(II Corinthians 4:2, BLB)

Sorrow

Disappointments in life bring sorrow. Prolonged sorrow can lead to depression. In Christ, there is newness of life. Rebuke the spirit of sorrow. Live life anew. The Lord has great things in store for you!

"And the ransomed of the LORD shall return, and come to Zion with songs and everlasting joy upon their heads: they shall obtain joy and gladness, and sorrow and sighing shall flee away."

(Isaiah 35:10, KJV)

Temptation

We all suffer temptation at one time or another and in one area or another. If you yield to temptation each time it tempts you, the harder it will be to turn away the next time. So, resist temptation, and watch the enemy flee from you.

"No temptation has overtaken you that is not common to man. God is faithful, and he will not let you be tempted beyond your ability, but with the temptation he will also provide the way of escape, that you may be able to endure it."

(I Corinthians 10:13, ESV)

Thievery

Do not take for yourself that which belongs to another. Tell the Lord what you have desire of and allow Him to provide for you in His own time.

"For out of the heart proceed evil thoughts, murders, adulteries, fornications, thefts, false witness, blasphemies."
(Matthew 15:19, KJV)

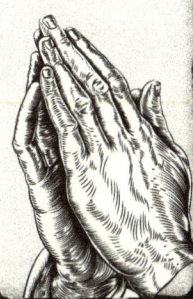

Tolerance

Each day, we may encounter people who are different from us. They may look differently, speak differently, think differently, and act differently. Regardless of how many differences you have from others, the amount of love and care you demonstrate towards them should not be impacted. The love of God must supersede all factors that tend to divide the human race.

"With all humility and gentleness, with patience, showing tolerance for one another in love."
(Ephesians 4:2, NASB)

Transgression

Give your transgressions over to the Lord. Remember, our transgressions do not define or own us, for we were bought with a price- the blood of Jesus. Walk in His grace, and <u>Rest in His goodness</u>.

"...made us alive with Christ even when we were dead in transgressions--it is by grace you have been saved."
(Ephesians 2:5, NLT)

Treasure

The treasures we store up for emergencies or a rainy day are only of value on earth. What treasures are you storing up in heaven? Are you storing up faithfulness, obedience, kindness, brotherly love, peace, gentleness, and longsuffering? Treasure these characteristics and exhibit them, and you will reap great rewards.

"Lay not up for yourselves treasures upon earth, where moth and rust doth corrupt, and where thieves break through and steal."

(Matthew 6:19, KJV)

Trust

Humans are fallible- prone to err. Conversely, God is infallible. So, if we are going to place complete trust in someone, would it not make more sense to completely trust the infallible God? <u>Rest in Him</u>- completely.

"Trust in the LORD with all thine heart; and lean not unto thine own understanding."
(Proverbs 3:5, KJV)

Trustworthy

Be a trustworthy confidante. Hold that which is dear to another in strict confidence as you would expect someone to do for you. Be honorable. Be upstanding. Be committed. Be someone that can be counted on.

"A gossip goes around telling secrets, but those who are trustworthy can keep a confidence."
(Proverbs 11:13, NLT)

Truth

Allow truth to guide your path, your behavior, your speech, your thoughts, and your actions. For assistance, read the Word of Truth, and allow it to permeate your being.

"However, when He, the Spirit of truth, has come, He will guide you into all truth; for He will not speak on His own authority, but whatever He hears He will speak; and He will tell you things to come."
(John 16:13, NKJV)

Value

From the moment you were conceived,
in the mind of God, you held value.
Remember, He made you to be just a little
lower that the angels, the heavenly hosts.
Do not allow the enemy to make you feel
worthless, for you were uniquely and
wonderfully designed.

*"But the very hairs of your head are all
numbered. Do not fear therefore;
you are of more value than
many sparrows."*
(Luke 12:7, NKJV)

Victorious

We engage in one battle at a time, and we are victorious in them all. The battles have already been won through Christ Jesus, our Lord and our Savior.

"For everyone who has been born of God overcomes the world. And this is the victory that has overcome the world —our faith."
(I John 5:4, ESV)

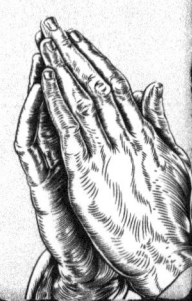

Victory

Because we are more than conquerors in Christ Jesus, we have already overcome all challenges that present themselves to us.

"But thanks be to God, which giveth us the victory through our Lord Jesus Christ."
(I Corinthians 15:57, KJV)

Weeping

Weeping is for but a season, but the joy of the Lord is everlasting! When the tears seem to flow continuously from your eyes, <u>Rest in Him</u>, knowing...

"For his anger lasts only a moment, but his favor lasts a lifetime; weeping may stay for the night, but rejoicing comes in the morning."
(Psalm 30:5, NIV)

Weakness

In our mortal bodies, weakness exists. However, our spirits are strong in the Lord. When the flesh and spirit war against one another, feed your spirit, so it may be victorious in all things.

"Watch and pray that you may not enter into temptation. The spirit indeed is willing, but the flesh is weak."
(Matthew 26:41, ESV)

Weary

Feeling tired, exhausted, despondent, or even overwhelmed is not uncommon for the average person. Be encouraged and continue to press toward the mark for the prize, and when needed, take your Rest in Him.

"And let us not be weary in well doing: for in due season we shall reap, if we faint not."
(Galatians 6:9, KJV)

Wickedness

Wickedness surrounds us on a daily basis. Nevertheless, we do not allow it to permeate our being. Remember, it is in the Lord that we move, live, and have our being, and wickedness has no place in the lives of the righteous.

"A person will not be established by wickedness, But the root of the righteous will not be moved."
(Proverbs 12:3, NASB)

Wonderful

No matter the challenges we encounter, we have a Savior who is wonderful and just. He will walk with us side by side, showing us the way. He is forever mindful of us.

"For unto us a child is born, unto us a son is given: and the government shall be upon his shoulder: and his name shall be called Wonderful, Counseller, The mighty God, The everlasting Father, The Prince of Peace."

(Isaiah 9:6, KJV)

Worry

Worrying is overrated and pays for nothing except sickness, heartache, stress, and high blood pressure. Remember, the Lord is not slack in His promises, and His Word will not return unto Him void. So, <u>Rest in Him</u>, and release your worries.

"Can any one of you by worrying add a single hour to your life?"

(Matthew 6:27, NIV)

Gift of Salvation for Non-Believers

"For all have sinned, and come short of the glory of God." (Romans 3:23)

This section was written especially for non-believers, those who have not accepted the gift of salvation. The gift of salvation saves souls from eternal damnation and is a free gift offered by God Himself.

John 3:16-18 says, *"For God so loved the world, that he gave his only begotten Son, that whosoever believeth in him should not perish, but have everlasting life. For God sent not his Son into the world to condemn the world; but that the world through him might be saved. He that believeth on him is not condemned: but he that believeth not is condemned already, because he hath not believed in the name of the only begotten Son of God."*

This section of scripture tells us God's purpose for giving His son Jesus to the world. The world was in a bad condition. The world was overwrought with sin; the people were living for fleshly desires rather than for God's desires.

As a result of the world's conditions, God decided He would offer the perfect sacrifice that would save the world from being a place where people were lost and had no hope. He decided His own son could stand in proxy for the sin-filled world, taking all sin upon Himself.

So Jesus came, born of a virgin, to save this dying world. He walked on this earth for 33 ½ years, doing the work of His Heavenly Father. At the appointed time, He died by way of crucifixion upon a cross at Calvary, on Golgotha's hill. He shed His blood and died for you and for me. Because His blood was pure, it paid the penalty for all unrighteousness and gave those who believe in Him direct access to His father's throne.

Scripture tells us in Matthew 27:51 that the veil of the temple was ripped in two from top to bottom, at the moment that Jesus' spirit left His body. As a result of the veil's removal, we are no longer required to have a high priest make intercession for us. We, as the children of the Most High God, are able to approach the throne of God for ourselves, and Jesus sits on the right hand of the Father making intercession for us.

But what is even more miraculous than God offering His own son as the perfect sacrifice was the fact that when Jesus was placed in grave clothes and placed in a tomb, He only remained there until the third day. God would not have it that His son would remain in the heart of the earth forever. In order for people to believe in the awesome power of God and His dear son Jesus, a miracle had to be performed. So, on the third day, after Jesus died on the cross, He was resurrected, demonstrating the omnipotence of God.

This very act was the act that would cause people to believe in a god that reigns supreme and holds the power of the universe in His very hands, a god that could save them from themselves.

Today, if you are an unbeliever, you can change your destiny. You can change where you will spend your eternity. Our Heavenly Father gives us the freedom of choice about how we want to live our life here on earth and how we want to spend eternity. In Deuteronomy 30:19, God boldly declares, *"I call heaven and earth to record this day against you, that I have set before you life and death, blessing and cursing: therefore choose life, that both thou and thy seed may live."*

So, dear friend what choice will you make today? Will you spend your eternity with the Creator or will you suffer Hell's eternal flames? Again, the choice is yours. Just as the men aboard the ship who were with Jonah became believers, you too can make a choice to accept the only one and true living God as your god.

If after reading the above passages, you have decided that you want to spend your eternity in Heaven with God, the creator, and His son Jesus, and the Holy Spirit, read through what has affectionately come to be known as the Roman's Road. This is the road to salvation. As you read through the scriptures that comprise the Roman's Road, you will also read the explanation for each scripture, so you will have clarity about what you are reading and confessing.

The Roman's Road to Salvation

The road to salvation begins with Romans 3:23 which declares, *"For all have sinned, and come short of the glory of God."* This scripture explains that everyone has come short of God's glory and needs redemption. Then, Romans 6:23a states, *"For the wages of sin is death."* Here, we learn that the consequence of living a life of sin is death. Everyone will experience physical death as a result of the sin committed in the garden of Eden, but those who commit themselves to a life of sin will suffer eternal damnation in the lake of fire (Rev. 19). Continue with the rest of verse 6:23 that says, *"but the gift of God is eternal life through Jesus Christ our Lord."* There is an alternative to suffering eternal damnation. We can accept the gift of salvation by accepting Jesus as our personal Lord and Savior. Then, Romans 5:8 says, *"But God commendeth his love toward us, in that, while we were yet sinners, Christ died for us."* We are able to receive the gift of salvation because Christ came to earth and shed His blood for us on the cross.

Continue to Romans 10: 9-10 which says, *"That if thou shalt confess with thy mouth the Lord Jesus, and shalt believe in thine heart that God hath raised him from the dead, thou shalt be saved. For with the heart man believeth unto righteousness; and with the mouth confession is made unto salvation."* If we confess with our mouths that Jesus is the son of God, that He came and died for our sins, and that God raised Him from the dead, we will receive salvation.

Finish with Romans 10:13, which states, *"For whosoever shall call upon the name of the Lord shall be saved."* Call upon the name of God by saying these words, **"Lord Jesus, come into my heart and save me, Lord. I believe that you are the Son of God who came and died on the cross for my sins. I believe that you rose from the grave. I also believe that you now sit in heaven on the right side of the Father, making intercession for me. I accept you as my Lord and my Savior."**

Now that you have confessed with your mouth that Jesus is the son of God and that He died for our sins and rose from the grave, **YOU ARE NOW SAVED!!!!** You will spend your eternity in heaven.

The next step is very important- you must find a Bible-based church that teaches the Word of God and confesses the Lord Jesus Christ to be the son of God. Don't delay. Do this immediately. Do not leave yourself open to the enemy. Get connected with the saints of the Most High God and keep yourself covered with the unspotted blood of the Lamb.

Here is my prayer for you.

Father God,

I thank you for the opportunity to minister your word to the unsaved, the unchurched, and the uncommitted. Father God, I pray now for the souls who have just received the gift of salvation. Lord Father, they have opened their hearts to you, and I know that you have received them into your kingdom and written their names in the Book of Life. Father God, I pray that you will touch their lives and show yourself mightily before them. Let their eyes be opened by the scales falling off, allowing them to see clearly.

Father God, I even pray for the backslider, those who have turned away from you after receiving the gift of salvation. You said in your Word that you desire that none would perish. So Lord, I send your Word to them right now, praying that they would confess the iniquity in their heart, repent, and turn from their evil ways, so that they may receive a life of abundance. You said in your Word in Matthew Chapter 14, that every knee shall bow before you and every tongue will confess that Jesus is Lord.

Father God, I pray now that we all come under subjection to your Word and that we will humbly submit our lives to you. I ask all these things in the name of my Lord and Savior Jesus Christ.
Amen, Amen, Amen!!!!

I will continue to pray for your success in your walk with God. Remember, this spiritual walk that you are about to embark on will not be an easy walk, but remember, the race is not given to the swift but to those who endure to the end.

Be blessed with heaven's best. I love you!

About the Author

Dr. Cassundra White-Elliott resides in California with her family, where as an English/Education professor, she teaches at various community colleges.

When writing, she composes with the direction of the Holy Spirit, in an effort to share with God's people all He has for them.

In addition to teaching and writing, Dr. Elliott also serves as an evangelistic teacher. She is also the founder of International Women's Commission, a ministry that serves the needs of the entire person, by attending to healing the mind, body, soul, and spirit.

Dr. Elliott holds a Ph.D. in Education, a Master's degree in English Composition, and a Bachelor's degree in Education.

Dr. Elliott is the founder and editor-in-chief for *Christian Inspiration* magazine, which covers topics germane to Christian living and the world at large.

Dr. Elliott is also the founder of CLF Publishing, LLC. For your publishing needs, go online to www.clfpublishing.org.

www.ingramcontent.com/pod-product-compliance
Lightning Source LLC
Chambersburg PA
CBHW032142040426
42449CB00005B/361